Quarterback Tom Brady

FOOTBALL'S GOAT ERA

Quarterback Drew Brees

NFL SUPER BOWL STORIES

FOOTBALL'S GOAT ERA

(2005–2014)

JAMES BARRY

Quarterback Peyton Manning

CREATIVE SPORTS

CREATIVE EDUCATION / CREATIVE PAPERBACKS

Published by Creative Education and Creative Paperbacks
P.O. Box 227, Mankato, Minnesota 56002
Creative Education and Creative Paperbacks are imprints of The Creative Company
www.thecreativecompany.us

Design and production by Blue Design (www.bluedes.com)
Art direction by Graham Morgan
Edited by Kremena Spengler

Images by Getty Images/Al Bello, 19, Al Messerschmidt, 4–5, 17, 32, Andy Hayt, 7, Chris Graythen, 20, Damian Strohmeyer, 9, Donald Miralle, 25, Elsa, 31, Focus On Sport, 6, George Rose, 7, Harry How, 30, Jed Jacobsohn, 11, JEFF HAYNES, 1, Jim McIsaac, 12, Jim Rogash, 15, Jon Soohoo, 6, 10, Justin Edmonds, 3, Michael Reaves, cover, Nick Laham, 29, Otto Greule Jr, 7, 10, Rob Tringali, 16, Robert Riger, 7, Robin Alam/Icon Sportswire, 6, Ronald Martinez, 2, Streeter Lecka, 26–27, Tom Hauck, 22; NFL/Vernon Biever, 6

Library of Congress Cataloging-in-Publication Data
Names: Barry, James, author.
Title: Football's goat era (2005–2014) / James Barry.
Description: Mankato, Minnesota : Creative Education and Creative Paperbacks, [2026] | Series: Creative sports: NFL super bowl stories | Includes index. | Audience: Ages 8–12 | Audience: Grades 4–6 | Summary: "Tom Brady, Peyton Manning, Drew Brees: Football's GOAT Era (2005–2014) was dominated by these names. Dramatic recaps introduce middle-grade readers to star NFL players from this era and ten exciting Super Bowls"– Provided by publisher.
Identifiers: LCCN 2024051461 (print) | LCCN 2024051462 (ebook) | ISBN 9798889896104 (library binding) | ISBN 9781682777763 (paperback) | ISBN 9798889896906 (ebook)
Subjects: LCSH: Football–United States–History–21st century–Juvenile literature. | National Football League–History–21st century–Juvenile literature.
Classification: LCC GV955.5.N35 B385 2026 (print) | LCC GV955.5.N35 (ebook) | DDC 796.332/6406–dc23/eng/20241121
LC record available at https://lccn.loc.gov/2024051461
LC ebook record available at https://lccn.loc.gov/2024051462

Printed in India

Quarterback Aaron Rodgers

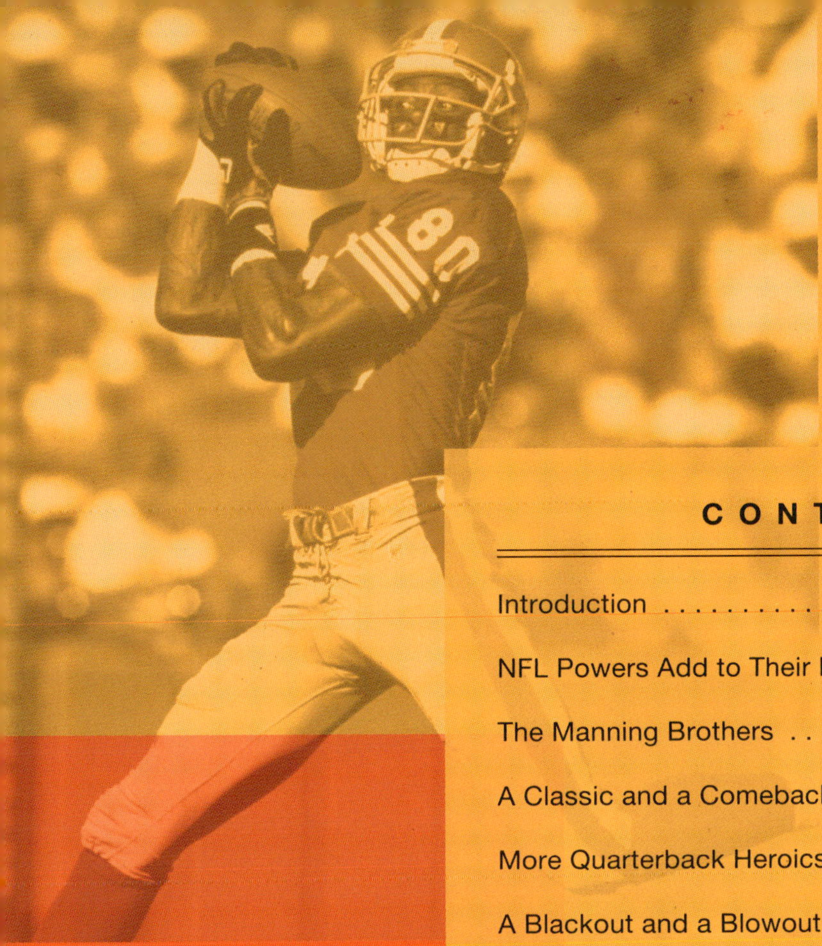

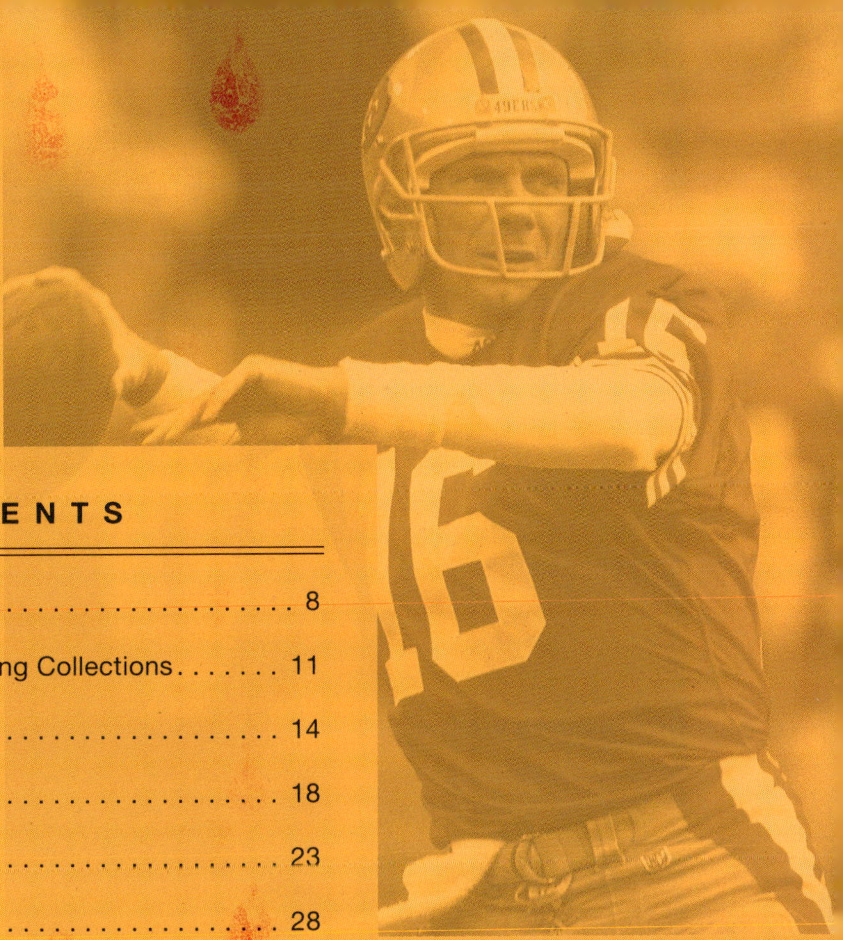

CONTENTS

Introduction 8

NFL Powers Add to Their Ring Collections 11

The Manning Brothers 14

A Classic and a Comeback 18

More Quarterback Heroics 23

A Blackout and a Blowout 28

Index 32

SUPER BOWL LEGENDS

Tom Brady 10

Peyton Manning 15

Eli Manning 16

Drew Brees 20

Aaron Rodgers 27

Bill Belichick 29

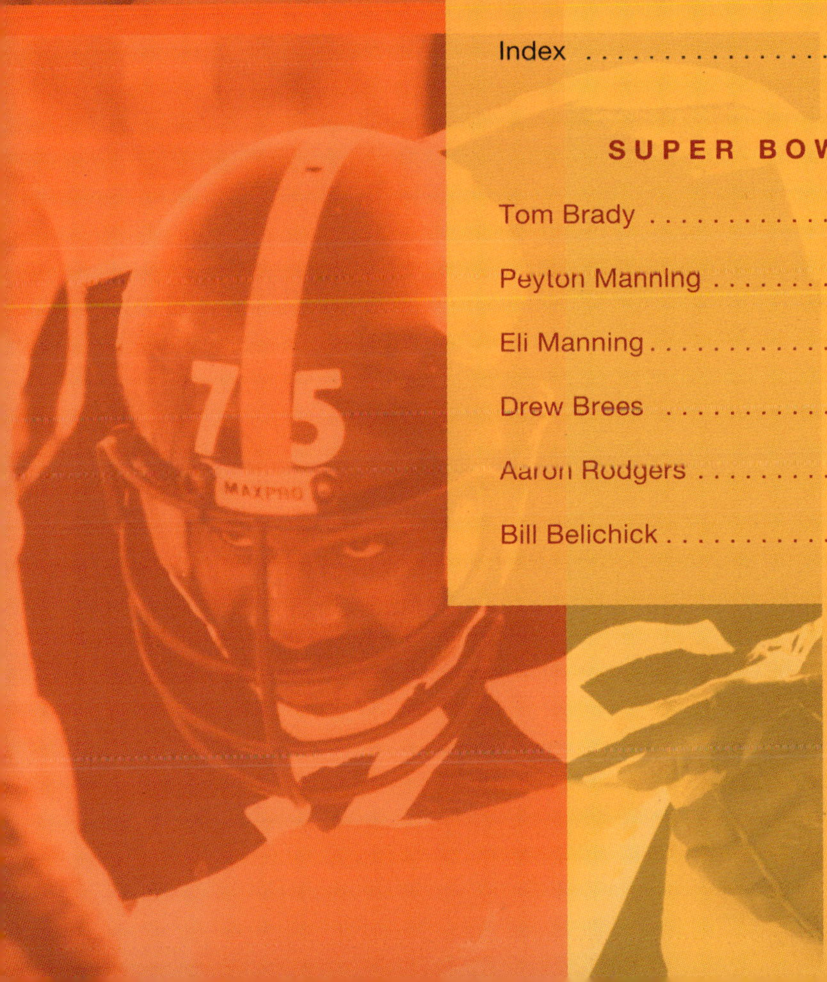

INTRODUCTION

It's the fourth quarter of Super Bowl XLII (42). There's one minute left on the clock. The New York Giants trail the New England Patriots by four points. It's third down and five. Eli Manning drops back to pass, and he's swarmed by defensive linemen. It looks like a sure sack. But he somehow escapes the pressure and throws up a prayer. Wide receiver David Tyree leaps for the deep ball and pins it against his helmet. It's a catch! A 32-yard gain! Two Manning completions later, the Giants take the lead. They become Super Bowl champions. They beat Tom Brady and the unbeaten Patriots. Manning becomes a legend of his own.

Every team in the National Football League (NFL) wants to win the Super Bowl. It's the championship game between the best teams from each conference. In the 2000s and the 2010s, great quarterbacks came to dominate the game. Their legendary names and heart-pounding plays tell the story of football's "GOAT Era."

Wide receiver David Tyree, Super Bowl XLIII (43)

QUARTERBACK
NEW ENGLAND PATRIOTS, 2000–2019;
TAMPA BAY BUCCANEERS, 2020–2022
6-FOOT-4, 225 POUNDS

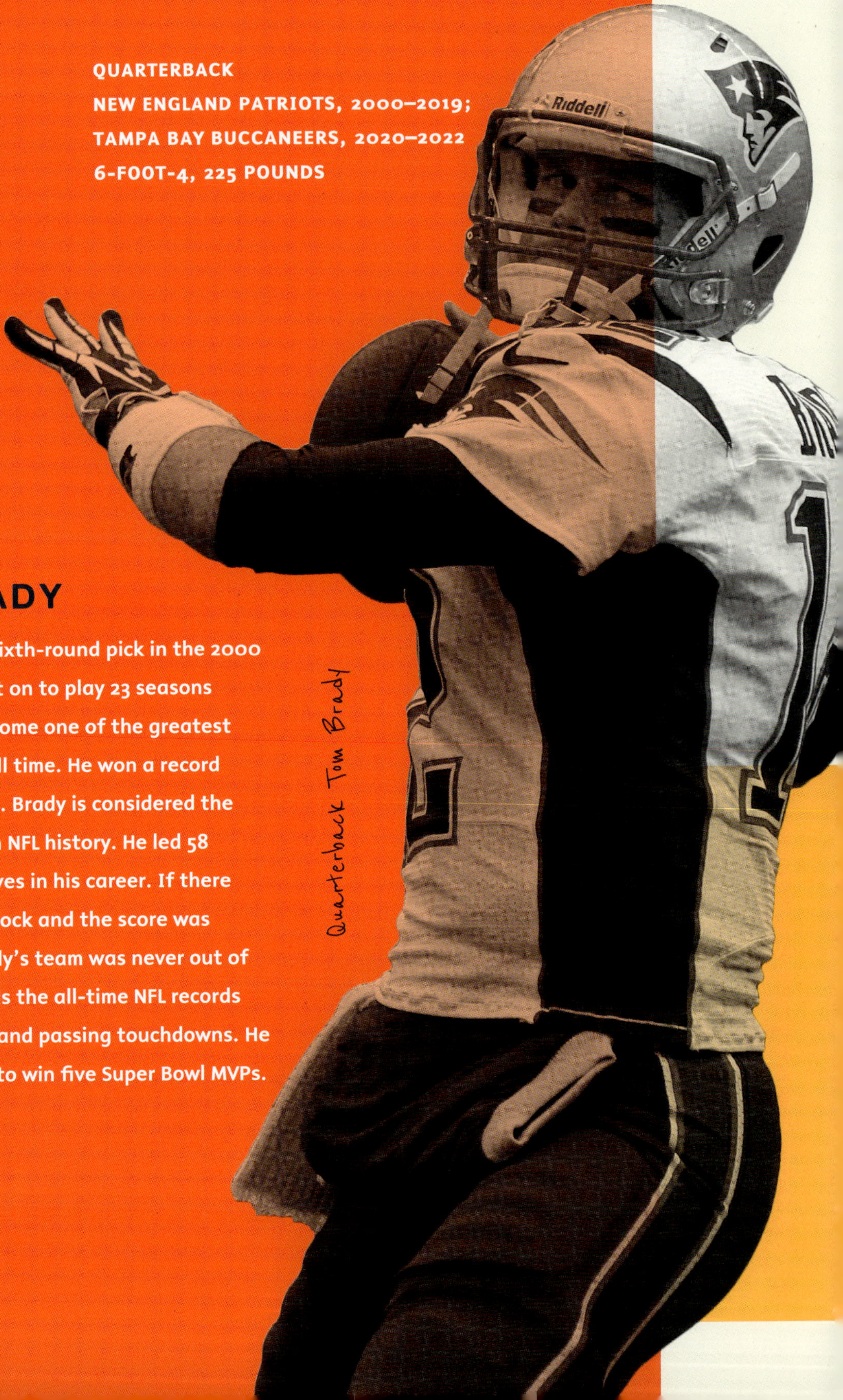

TOM BRADY

Tom Brady was a sixth-round pick in the 2000 NFL Draft. He went on to play 23 seasons in the NFL and become one of the greatest quarterbacks of all time. He won a record seven Super Bowls. Brady is considered the greatest winner in NFL history. He led 58 game-winning drives in his career. If there was time on the clock and the score was within reach, Brady's team was never out of the game. He holds the all-time NFL records for passing yards and passing touchdowns. He is the only player to win five Super Bowl MVPs.

Quarterback Tom Brady

Linebacker Tedy Bruschi sacks quarterback Donovan McNabb.

NFL POWERS ADD TO THEIR RING COLLECTIONS

Super Bowl XXXIX (39) was a matchup between the New England Patriots and the Philadelphia Eagles. The Patriots were looking to defend their Super Bowl title. They were led by head coach Bill Belichick and star quarterback Tom Brady. They were a force in the American Football Conference (AFC). The Eagles had finally reached the Super Bowl after three straight losses in the National Football Conference (NFC) Championship Game. They were led by head coach Andy Reid and quarterback Donovan McNabb.

The two teams met at Alltel Stadium in Jacksonville, Florida. The Eagles struck first in the second quarter. McNabb threw a touchdown pass to tight end L. J. Smith. Brady answered with a touchdown pass of his own. The score was 7–7 at halftime. The Patriots took the lead on their first possession of the second half. The drive ended with another Brady touchdown pass. McNabb and the Eagles tied it up again later in the quarter. The Eagles were right in it.

7
Wilson

But the Patriots started the fourth quarter with two straight scoring drives. They led 24–14. McNabb tried his best, throwing 20 passes in the last quarter. The 10-point lead proved too much to overcome. Brady and the Patriots were too steady. It was their third Super Bowl victory in four seasons. They were on top of the football world.

The Pittsburgh Steelers faced the Seattle Seahawks in Super Bowl XL (40). The Steelers were a historic franchise seeking their fifth Super Bowl title. The Steelers were led by head coach Bill Cowher and young quarterback Ben Roethlisberger. The Seahawks had reached their first Super Bowl in team history. They were led by head coach Mike Holmgren and star running back Shaun Alexander. He set a league record with 27 rushing touchdowns and was named the NFL's Most Valuable Player (MVP).

The two teams met at Ford Field in Detroit, Michigan. After a slow first quarter, the Seahawks led 3–0. Late in the second quarter, Roethlisberger connected with wide receiver Hines Ward for a 37-yard completion. It brought the Steelers to the three-yard line. Two plays later, Roethlisberger ran it into the endzone. Pittsburgh led 7–3 at halftime. On the second play of the second half, Steelers running back Willie Parker broke the game open. He stormed through the Seattle defense for a Super Bowl record 75-yard rushing touchdown.

Early in the fourth quarter, Seattle was driving with a chance to take the lead. It was third and long. Pittsburgh cornerback Ike Taylor intercepted Matt Hasselbeck's pass and returned it for 24 yards. A few plays later, Steelers wide receiver Antwaan Randle El made Super Bowl history. He

Quarterback Ben Roethlisberger

became the first wide receiver to throw a touchdown pass in the big game. Pittsburgh led 21–10, and the score never changed. The Steelers were Super Bowl champions for the fifth time.

THE MANNING BROTHERS

Super Bowl XLI (41) was a matchup between the Indianapolis Colts and the Chicago Bears. Both teams were playing for their second Super Bowl victory. The Bears were led by their defense, featuring great players like linebackers Brian Urlacher and Lance Briggs. The Colts were led by star quarterback Peyton Manning and their high-powered offense. The Bears' Lovie Smith and the Colts' Tony Dungy became the first Black head coaches to coach in the Super Bowl.

The two teams met at Dolphin Stadium in Miami. It was the first Super Bowl played in the rain. The game kicked off with a bang. Bears wide receiver Devin Hester returned the opening kickoff 92 yards for a touchdown. It was the quickest score in Super Bowl history. But Manning answered with a 53-yard touchdown pass. The Colts led 16–14 at halftime.

The most important play of the game came early in the fourth quarter. The Bears had the ball with a chance to take the lead. Rex Grossman had just completed a 22-yard pass to wide receiver Muhsin Muhammad. He dropped back and threw another one to Muhammad. But it was intercepted by Colts defensive

PEYTON MANNING

Peyton Manning was the first overall pick in the 1998 NFL Draft. He went on to become one of the greatest quarterbacks in NFL history. He is the only player to win five NFL MVP awards. Manning holds all kinds of NFL records, including the most passing yards and the most passing touchdowns in a single season. He's known as one of the smartest quarterbacks ever. After missing a season with a neck injury, he revived his career with the Denver Broncos. He won his second Super Bowl with Denver. He played a total of 17 seasons in the NFL.

QUARTERBACK
INDIANAPOLIS COLTS, 1998–2010
DENVER BRONCOS, 2012–2015
6-FOOT-5, 230 POUNDS

QUARTERBACK
NEW YORK GIANTS
2004–2019
6-FOOT-5, 220 POUNDS

ELI MANNING

The younger brother of Peyton, Eli Manning built his own legacy in the NFL. He was the first overall pick in the 2004 NFL Draft. He played all 16 seasons of his career with the New York Giants. He was a quarterback who always played his best in the biggest moments. Manning and the Giants faced the powerful New England Patriots twice in the Super Bowl. New York was the underdog both times. Both times Manning stepped up when his team needed him most. His game-winning drives in those two Super Bowls are the stuff of NFL history.

back Kelvin Hayden, who returned it 56 yards for a touchdown. Indianapolis took a 29–17 lead, and that was the score when the game ended. The Colts were Super Bowl champions. Peyton Manning had finally won his first title. He earned Super Bowl MVP to go along with it.

Linebacker Brian Urlacher

Super Bowl XLII (42) saw the Patriots return to the big game. This time they faced the New York Giants, led by quarterback Eli Manning. The Patriots entered the game with a perfect record. They were the first team to go undefeated in a 16-game season. Brady won his first NFL MVP and set a then-NFL record with 50 passing touchdowns. The Patriots were huge favorites to win the game. The Giants were considered lucky to be there.

The two teams met at University of Phoenix Stadium in Glendale, Arizona. The Giants started the game with a long scoring drive that ended in a field goal. The Patriots answered with a touchdown drive of their own. New England led 7–3 early in the second quarter. Both defenses were playing well. The score remained 7–3 until the fourth quarter. Then Manning threw a deep ball to David Tyree who caught it for a 32-yard gain. After two more completions, the Giants clinched the victory at 17–14. New York did it! It was one of the biggest upsets in NFL history. The Giants were Super Bowl champions, and Manning was named Super Bowl MVP.

A CLASSIC AND A COMEBACK

Super Bowl XLIII (43) was a matchup between a recent champion and a surprise contender. It was the powerful Steelers versus the Arizona Cardinals. Pittsburgh's defense allowed the fewest yards and the fewest points in the regular season. Fierce linebacker James Harrison was named the NFL Defensive Player of the Year. The Cardinals were playing in their first Super Bowl. They were led by 37-year-old quarterback Kurt Warner.

The two teams met at Raymond James Stadium in Tampa, Florida. The Cardinals were down 10–7 late in the second quarter. They were on the goal line with 18 seconds left in the first half. Warner threw a short pass to Anquan Boldin, but it was intercepted by Harrison. The big linebacker returned it 100 yards for a touchdown to end the half. It was a Super Bowl record. The Cardinals went to the locker room in shock. The Steelers led 17–7.

The score was 20–7 entering the fourth quarter. Then the Cardinals scored 16 straight points. They led 23–20. There were less than three minutes left. Roethlisberger led his team down the field. He found wide receiver Santonio Holmes for several big completions. With less than a minute left, Roethlisberger found Holmes again. This time, it was a touchdown in the back of the endzone. The Steelers retook the lead and won 27–23. It was their sixth Super Bowl title. The game would go down as one of the greatest in NFL history.

Linebacker James Harrison

QUARTERBACK
NEW ORLEANS SAINTS
2006–2020
6-FOOT-0, 209 POUNDS

DREW BREES

Drew Brees was a second-round pick in the 2001 NFL Draft. Many NFL teams thought he was too short and his arm was too weak. He became one of the greatest quarterbacks in NFL history. He holds the record for back-to-back games with a touchdown pass at 54 games. He's second all-time in passing yards and passing touchdowns. He led the NFL in passing yards seven times in his career. Brees was one of the game's great leaders. He was known for his pre-game speeches, motivating his teammates before kickoff. He led the New Orleans Saints to their first Super Bowl.

The Colts returned to Super Bowl XLIV (44) to face the New Orleans Saints. It was the Saints' first Super Bowl appearance. They were led by head coach Sean Payton and quarterback Drew Brees. Their offense led the league in scoring. Peyton Manning was still the captain of the Colts' offense. He won another NFL MVP. They were the league's two best teams, but most people expected the Colts to win.

The two teams met at Sun Life Stadium in Miami, Florida. The Colts scored the first 10 points of the game. But the Saints crept back. The score was 10–6 at halftime. Coach Payton made a big decision to start the second half. He called for an onside kick instead of a regular kickoff. The Saints recovered it! It was a bold move, and it paid off. Brees led the Saints on a touchdown drive.

But Indianapolis took a 17–16 lead into the fourth quarter. Colts kicker Matt Stover missed a 51-yard field goal. Then Brees ended another perfect drive with a touchdown pass. The Saints led 24–17. Manning led the Colts into Saints territory. But when he tried to find wide receiver Reggie Wayne, he was intercepted. Cornerback Tracy Porter picked it off and returned it 74 yards for a touchdown. The game was sealed. New Orleans won by a score of 31–17. The Saints won their first ever Super Bowl. Brees was the clear Super Bowl MVP. He became a hero in New Orleans.

MORE QUARTERBACK HEROICS

Super Bowl XLV (45) was a matchup between two teams with rich histories of winning. It was the Steelers versus the Green Bay Packers. Both teams had great defenses. The Steelers allowed the fewest points in the regular season, and the Packers allowed the second fewest. Roethlisberger was still the leader of Pittsburgh's offense. Green Bay's offense was captained by quarterback Aaron Rodgers. It was expected to be a close game.

The two teams met at Cowboys Stadium in Arlington, Texas. The Packers struck first. Rodgers threw a pass to wide receiver Jordy Nelson for a 29-yard touchdown. Roethlisberger threw an interception on the very first play of the next drive. Packers safety Nick Collins returned it 37 yards for a touchdown. The Packers scored twice within 20 seconds. They led 21–10 at halftime.

The Steelers scored another touchdown early in the third quarter. It was 21–17. The game was within reach. The Steelers had the ball to start the fourth quarter. Packers linebacker Clay Matthews tackled running back Rashard Mendenhall in the backfield. Matthews forced a fumble, and the Packers recovered. Rodgers made Pittsburgh pay again. He led his team down the field and completed his third touchdown pass of the game. He rose to the moment in his first Super Bowl. The Packers won by a score of 31–25. Rodgers finished with more than 300 passing

Quarterback Aaron Rodgers

yards and three touchdowns. He was named Super Bowl MVP. Another all-time great quarterback had led his team to glory. Football's GOAT Era was in full swing.

Super Bowl XLVI (46) was a rematch between the Patriots and the Giants. Once again it was Belichick and Brady leading New England to the Super Bowl. Brady had another fantastic year, throwing for more than 5,000 yards. Eli Manning was still leading New York's offense. He had a strong trio of wide receivers in Victor Cruz, Hakeem Nicks, and Mario Manningham.

The two teams met at Lucas Oil Stadium in Indianapolis, Indiana. The game was close the whole way. The Patriots led 17–15 after three quarters. It would come down to the fourth. One of the key plays of the game came around the four-minute mark. The Patriots had the ball just past midfield. It was second and long. Brady threw a high pass to an open Wes Welker, who missed the leaping catch. The ball passed right through his fingers. New England ended up punting.

On the first play of the next drive, Manning made one of the greatest throws in Super Bowl history. He threw a bomb down the left sideline, perfectly placed in Manningham's hands. It was a huge 38-yard gain. It became the play fans would never forget. After a few more big completions, Giants running back Ahmad Bradshaw ran for a touchdown with a minute left. Brady and the Patriots were unable to score in the final minute. The Giants had taken down the mighty Patriots again. They won by a score of 21–17. Eli Manning won his second Super Bowl MVP.

Quarterback Tom Brady

XLII
BRADY
12
PATRIOTS

QUARTERBACK
GREEN BAY PACKERS
2005–2022
6-FOOT-2, 223 POUNDS

AARON RODGERS

Aaron Rodgers didn't start a game until his fourth season in the NFL. He sat behind Packers legend Brett Favre until his time came. Then he became one of the best quarterbacks the game has seen. Rodgers won four NFL MVP awards with the Packers. He led them to victory in Super Bowl XLV (45) and was named Super Bowl MVP. He's known as one of the greatest throwers ever. He still has the highest career passer rating in NFL history. No great quarterback has ever avoided interceptions like Rodgers. He always stood out for his accuracy and his talent.

A BLACKOUT AND A BLOWOUT

The Baltimore Ravens faced the San Francisco 49ers in Super Bowl XLVII (47). It was the first time two brothers coached against each other in a Super Bowl. Jim Harbaugh was the 49ers' head coach, and John Harbaugh was the head coach of the Ravens.

The two teams met at the Mercedes-Benz Superdome in New Orleans, Louisiana. Ravens quarterback Joe Flacco kept up his great play in the first half. He threw three touchdown passes. The Ravens led 21–6 at halftime. Then Ravens wide receiver Jacoby Jones broke the game open. He returned the kickoff 108 yards for a touchdown. It seemed like Baltimore couldn't lose. Then the power in the stadium failed. It remained out for more than 30 minutes. The unexpected break seemed to give the 49ers life.

San Francisco scored two touchdowns within a few minutes. Ravens running back Ray Rice fumbled just a few plays later. It led to a San Francisco field goal. Just like that, the Ravens' lead was reduced. The score was 28–23. The 49ers had stormed back. A Ravens field goal made it an eight-point lead. Quarterback Colin Kaepernick ran for a 15-yard touchdown just a few minutes later. It was a two-point game. But the 49ers tried a two-point conversion and failed. The Ravens added another field goal and held on to their lead. They won by a final score of 34–31. Flacco was named Super Bowl MVP. He was the fourth quarterback in a row to win the award.

HEAD COACH
NEW ENGLAND PATRIOTS
2000–2023

BILL BELICHICK

Bill Belichick coached the New England Patriots to nine Super Bowl appearances and six victories. No other head coach has won six Super Bowls. He was the first coach to win three Super Bowls in a four-year span. Belichick also served as the team's general manager for many years. The Patriots reached a special level of consistency under his reign. They won at least 10 games for 17 seasons in a row. No other team has come close to that. Belichick was always known for his attention to detail. He is widely considered one of the greatest coaches of all time.

BOLDIN
81

Quarterback Russell Wilson

Super Bowl XLVIII (48) saw the Denver Broncos face the Seattle Seahawks. It was a matchup between the league's top offense and its top defense. The Broncos set an NFL record for points scored in a regular season. The attack was led by Peyton Manning. He continued his great career in Denver. He threw for 5,477 yards and 55 touchdowns—both NFL records. It was a historic season for Denver. But the Seahawks defense allowed the fewest points and the fewest yards in the regular season. They forced the most turnovers. It was set to be a great game.

The two teams met at MetLife Stadium in East Rutherford, New Jersey. From the first play, it was all Seahawks. A Broncos fumble led to a safety just seconds into the game. Seattle added two field goals in the first quarter. Then Manning threw two interceptions. The second one was returned 69 yards by linebacker Malcolm Smith for a touchdown. Just like that, the Seahawks led 22–0 at halftime.

When Seahawks wide receiver Percy Harvin returned the opening kickoff of the second half 87 yards for a touchdown, everyone knew it was over. It was the biggest Super Bowl blowout in years. Seattle won by a final score of 43–8. The Seahawks defense shut down the best regular-season offense of all time. Peyton Manning had another regular-season MVP, but he left the season with another Super Bowl loss. With that, football's GOAT Era came to an end.

Wide receiver Anquan Boldin

INDEX

Alexander, Shaun, 13
Arizona Cardinals, 18
Belichick, Bill, 11, 24, 29
Brady, Tom, 1, 8, 10, 11, 13, 17, 24, 25
Brees, Drew, 2, 20, 21
Chicago Bears, 14
Cowher, Bill, 13
Denver Broncos, 15, 31
Dungy, Tony, 14
Flacco, Joe, 28
fumble, 23, 31
Green Bay Packers, 23, 26, 27
Grossman, Rex, 14
Harrison, James, 18, 19
Hayden, Kelvin, 14
Hester, Devin, 14
Holmes, Santonio, 18
Indianapolis Colts, 14, 15, 17, 21, 24
interception, 13, 14, 18, 21, 23, 27, 31
Jones, Jacoby, 28
Manning, Eli, 8, 16, 17, 24
Manning, Peyton, 3, 14, 15, 16, 17, 21, 31
Manningham, Mario, 24
McNabb, Donovan, 11, 13
New England Patriots, 8, 10, 11, 13, 16, 17, 24, 29
New Orleans Saints, 20, 21, 28
New York Giants, 8, 16, 17, 24
onside kick, 21
Parker, Willie, 13
Payton, Sean, 21
Philadelphia Eagles, 11
Pittsburgh Steelers, 13, 14, 18, 23
Reid, Andy, 11,
Rodgers, Aaron, 5, 22, 23, 27
Roethlisberger, Ben, 12, 13, 18, 23
Seattle Seahawks, 13, 31
Smith, Lovie, 14
Tyree, David, 8, 9, 17
underdog, 16
Urlacher, Brian, 14, 17
Ward, Hines, 13
Welker, Wes, 24